T0003234

LETTERS
AROUND
A GARDEN

THE FRENCH LIST

Rilke in the garden of Muzot, undated, source unknown.

Rainer Maria Rilke

LETTERS
AROUND
A GARDEN

Translated from the French
with an Introduction by
WILL STONE

LONDON NEW YORK CALCUTTA

Seagull Books, 2024

First published in French as *Lettres autour d'un Jardin*
by La Délirante, Paris, 1977

The original works of Rainer Maria Rilke (1875–1926)
are in the public domain

First published in English translation by Seagull Books, 2024

Drawing of the leaves by Sam Szafran reproduced
with the kind permission of Lilette Szafran

ISBN   978 1 8030 9 334 5

British Library Cataloguing-in-Publication Data
A catalogue record for this book is available from the British Library

Typeset by Seagull Books, Calcutta, India
Printed and bound in the USA by Integrated Books International

Here yet is the hour that silvers
fused with gentle evening, pure metal
and which adds to the slow beauty
the slow returns of a musical tranquillity.

The old earth recovers and transforms;
a pure star outlives our labours.
scattered sounds, departing the day, fall in
and all return into the voice of the waters.

R. M. R.

From *Les Quatrains Valaisans*, 1924

(Translation by Will Stone)

CONTENTS

ACKNOWLEDGEMENTS

I would like to express my gratitude to the Canton Valais and Kulturstiftung Raron for awarding the translation residency in the Zentriegenhaus Raron during autumn 2022, where these letters finally made their way into the English language. I would also like to give thanks and acknowledge the debt owed to the Fondation Rilke in Sierre, and particularly to its director Brigitte Duvillard, who first drew my attention to the letters and generously lent her counsel on the texts and supporting material. I would also like to thank her colleague Sara In-Albon for her kind assistance in compiling the notes.

I should also like to acknowledge the important books on Rilke and Muzot written by Valais author Maurice Zermatten (1910–2001), namely, *Les années Valaisannes de Rilke* (1951) and *Les dernières années de Rainer Maria Rilke* (1975), as well as the more recent valuable account

Rilke en Valais (2021) by Jean-Michel Henny which I have drawn on for my introduction to this book.

The drawing by French artist Sam Szafran (1934–2019) is published with the kind permission of Lilette Szafran.

I dedicate these translations to the memory of my father Walter Ernest Stone (1929–2020) who accompanied me as co-driver on my first visit to Muzot, thence Raron, in 1996.

Will Stone

A NOTE ON THE FRENCH TEXT

Antoinette de Bonstetten guarded the letters from her correspondence with Rilke for half a century until late in life when she entrusted them to the owner of a French publishing house La Délirante in Paris. The letters were duly published in 1977 as *Lettres autour d'un Jardin* and have since appeared in successive editions.

INTRODUCTION

I. *The Road to Muzot*

In the year 1919, in a Europe exhausted by conflict and its concurrent diaspora, the poet Rainer Maria Rilke could be considered a stateless person, or *Heimatlos*, with no fixed centre of gravity. So Switzerland, the erstwhile sanctuary for Europe's disaffected writers, artists and pacifists during the war years, willingly presented itself as a potential haven which could fill the void. Rilke, inveterate traveller and hermitage seeker par excellence, was experiencing, at the age of forty-four, a growing need to sequester himself once again, but now to establish a sense of rootedness, such as he had known only in Paris, in the hope of re-encountering the creative élan which had deserted him after the prolonged trauma and dislocation engendered by the war. Paris, both sanctuary and crucible for his breakthrough *New Poems* (1907–08) and *Notebooks of Malte Laurids Brigge* (1910), had yet to restore its internationalist equilibrium after the war, and the wound still felt raw; the Paris flat in the rue Campagne Première which he was forced to flee in 1914 as an enemy alien, abandoning all his belongings in the process, had not only been reoccupied but the former occupant's possessions, including precious books and manuscripts, had also been sold off.

On a visit to Switzerland from Bavaria in June 1919, Rilke suddenly became trapped; he could no longer return to Munich as he had intended due to an abrupt change in the German immigration law. Lacking any viable alternatives, he was obliged to remain in the landlocked neutral country. The following two years saw the poet on a seemingly never-ending tour of Switzerland's regions and cities, educating himself on the country's culture and history while keeping one eye open for a potential dwelling place. It is astonishing and revealing just how much Rilke crammed into the months from June 1919 in his quest to secure a refuge until his long-term residence at the chateau of Berg-am-Irchel in Canton Zurich in November of that year. From June to September, he was not only in Zurich but also enjoyed visits or longer sojourns in Bern, Nyon, Geneva, Lausanne, Sils Baselgia in the Engadine, and Soglio in the Val Bragaglia below.

After some encouragement, he embarked on a highly successful lecture tour between the end of October and the end of November, opening in Zurich, then taking in St Gallen, Lucerne, Basel, Bern and Winterthur. From the beginning of December, he was installed in cosmopolitan Locarno on Lake Maggiore. And the following year, after leaving Locarno at the end of February, he repaired to Schönenberg in Canton Zurich to see in the spring, heading to Venice in early summer, back to Schönenberg for a brief spell, then travelling again in Switzerland over the remainder of the summer and into autumn. The month of October 1920 alone saw him visit Geneva, Bern, Sion and Sierre. A break in Paris, and then he was back revisiting Geneva and Basel in November.

However, all the time Rilke was discerning the landscapes and cities that communicated most intimately to him, bookmarking those to which he would return. The grandiose majesty and cold Nietzschean anonymity of the High Alps were not for Rilke, and the popular touristic stations and Alpine chintz were anathema; in contrast, it was the lower-lying landscapes that appealed to him. Eventually, it was the gentler, more companionable viticulture landscape of the Valais along the valley of the Rhone—an area he was unaware of until a Swiss friend drew his attention to it—that spoke most powerfully to him.

Rilke had first encountered the Canton Valais in October 2020. This rural landscape of vineyards and meadows adorning the steep slopes of the Rhone valley, a haven as yet undisturbed by the materialist modern world, made an admirable impression that remained with him. From mid-November, Rilke had begun a long winter residence at Berg-am-Irchel in Canton Zurich, courtesy of a beneficent countess. Now, as spring beckoned, the poet was obliged to move on. Once again Rilke's burgeoning contacts in Switzerland solved his looming vagrancy, the prieuré d'Etoy, midway along the northern Swiss shore of lac Léman (or Lake Geneva), would provide lodgings until the end of June. Here Rilke could gaze out across the vast lake to the Alpine massif rising above the Haute Savoie on its southern side, receive visits from the likes of the Princess Marie Thurn und Taxis or the poet Countess Anna de Noailles, and honour invitations to dine with the Swiss-French writer-biographer Guy de Pourtalès who happened to occupy rooms in the chateau next door.

Rilke's then partner, Baladine Klossowska, or 'Merline' as Rilke called her, was anxious to leave Berlin and join him at Berg, then later at Etoy. Both were aware that the cardinal purpose of Rilke's Swiss wanderings was to track down an anchorage. But in letters exchanged through May 1921, they fretted over what this destination might be, for though Merline wanted to stay with Rilke, she was nonetheless fully aware that this must be primarily *his* creative enclosure and that, as ever, the poet's vocation was sacrosanct. Merline spoke of her intention to go to Ticino, but Rilke seemed set on Sierre. On 11 June he excitedly pens from Rolle: 'Come, come, come! . . . Your idea of Muzzano is perhaps justified, yet it can't dislodge the vision within me which remains so powerful of Sierre, it is there I see us with such assurance that I almost believe we must be there.'[1] Merline was finally persuaded and she joined Rilke at Etoy on 19 June. On the 23rd they left for Sierre, checked into the Hotel Bellevue in the centre of the old town, and immediately began looking for a cheaper alternative.

They searched in vain; a little house in Sierre was offered, another in Sion, none seemed right; then a medieval tower at Goubing which seemed ideal but alas was occupied. Their despondency grew. Almost at the point of a melancholy departure from Sierre, Rilke, while returning

---

1 Rainer Maria Rilke and Baladine Klossowska, *Rainer Maria Rilke et Merline: Correspondance, 1920–1926* (Zurich: Editions Max Niehans, 1954), p. 361.

from the train station with their tickets, happened to shelter from a rainstorm beneath the shop blinds when in a window he spied a postcard showing a medieval chateau, a slender tower situated in a place called Muzot above the town; it stated 'for sale or rent'. Muzot? He had never heard of it. He soon learned it was pronounced 'Musotte'. The advert invited visits, so they went right away, a stiff climb up a winding lane from the town, to find the high wooden cross and the solitary poplar announcing the thirteenth-century tower perched above its vineyard and enclosed by low grey stone walls. A little way up the lane was a pictur-esque ancient chapel that lay abandoned. In this unforeseen moment, all suddenly seemed to fit and the entranced new-comers stood inside the old tower sensing here was a resi-dence fit for a poet. The history of the ancient building fascinated them: the noble Vaudois family of Blonay and then the Monthéis clan had left their marks; ghosts were even in residence.

And there had been helpful modernizations. In 1903, the by-then-dilapidated tower had been bought for 1,200 francs by a local businessman, M. Raunier, as a working-project pied-à-terre. This gentleman spent considerable time and money on salvaging the near ruins and making them habitable again, installing an outer staircase and porch, two balconies, and a garden on three sides. Now his widow, Mme Raunier, was ailing and the family were letting it go. But how to acquire it? Fate played its hand again, for one of Rilke's Swiss friends and patrons, the wealthy art collector Werner Reinhart of Winterthur, already happened to be a secret admirer of the little castle; when Rilke approached him, Reinhart saw the opportunity as an intervention of fate and immediately offered to rent it for the poet. In May 2022, he succeeded in purchasing the tower which ensured the security, the permanence Rilke sought. Rilke moved in as the new 'chatelain' on 26 July 1921, and through the summer, with Merline's inspired touch, furnishings, curtains and judicious decoration enhanced the living conditions in the austere and primitive tower. In the autumn, the poet and the artist parted after a halcyon summer of intense companionship, and Baladine returned to Berlin, distraught at the separation she knew had to come despite Rilke's lofty assurances of their continued entente. Rilke would spend his first winter alone in Muzot but for his discreet housekeeper Mlle Baumgartner, until the emergence of the Valaisan spring proved a catalyst to a creative epiphany. There is a hint of what that might bring in a letter from 31 December 1921 to the daughter of M. Raunier, in which we see Rilke's preoccupation with resuming serious work after the years of perpetual adjournment:

> Your old Muzot greets you as I do; the old manor seems happy to be heated and assiduously inhabited . . . I do hope you can join us for tea one day, but I am presently (after my drawn-out preparations) engaged in work that I should not like to interrupt even for a moment. It is so long since I enjoyed such calm and I have to renew so many threads broken during the terrible years.[2]

Rilke was bewitched by the Valais landscape, which to him represented a beguiling marriage of Provence and Spain, with each walk along vineyard terraces and sun-baked lanes summoning memories of earlier travels. The most revealing letter of his first impressions is that of 25 July 1921 to Princess Thurn und Taxis:

> [W]hat strange magic these places have exerted on me . . . ever since I saw them for the first-time last year during the time of the grape harvest. The fact that this countryside is an uncanny fusion of Spain

---

2 Maurice Zermatten, *Der Ruf der Stille*: *Rilkes Walliser Jahre* [The call of silence: Rilke's Valais years] (Zurich: Rascher Verlag, 1954), pp. 42–43.

and Provence, had struck me forcefully, for these two landscapes had enchanted me during the years before the war with an intensity unsurpassed by any others. And to now find their two voices reunited in a broad Alpine valley in Switzerland. And this unison does not lie just in the imagination. I have since learned that certain flowers grow here that one only finds in Provence and Spain. And the same goes for the butterflies. Thus, the soul of a great river (and the Rhone has always seemed to me one of the most astonishing) bears gifts and affinities across countries.[3]

Rilke adopted a semi-monastic existence, willingly interrupted by visits from friends, writers, artists and musicians, social intermissions which could dominate the finer months. Assisted by the loyal Nanny Wunderly-Volkart, who had also helped with the tenure at Berg-am-Irchel, and Mlle Baumgartner, Rilke was free to observe the nature around him and absorb the rural life whose centuries-old customs played out in accord with the seasons, often conversing with the local farmers and vine workers who lead

3 Rainer Maria Rilke and Marie von Thurn und Taxis, *Briefwechsel, Zweiter Band* [Correspondence, VOL. 2] (Zurich: Editions Max Niehans / Wiesbaden: Insel Verlag, 1951), pp. 672–80.

their donkeys with bulging baskets of grapes across the meadows. The local workers in turn had a sympathetic respect for this solitary man often seen descending to Sierre for his post or out on his walks, jotting observations in a little notebook. Long treks in the surrounding hills and vineyards, in the dense pine forests of Fjin, and along the glaucous blue-grey waters of the Rhone, pilgrimages to solitary chapels with their rustic Madonnas, or excursions further afield to the chateau de Tourbillon and basilica de Valère at Sion established a new sense of continuity and recurrence for the poet, gradually re-equipping him with the much-deferred inner equilibrium.

As he settled in at Muzot, at the forefront of Rilke's mind were the *Elegies*, consolidated in an unexpected surge of inspiration in 1912 while installed at the invitation of Princess Marie Thurn und Taxis in the castle of Duino on the Adriatic coast. The castle, seriously damaged by bombs during the war, was now under repair and the *Elegies* too needed to undergo a regeneracy, for the first half remained like a road once promising a great destination that had ended abruptly due to a landslip, shorn off by powerful external forces. The fragmental *Elegies* had become a weight that increased with the passing years and their creator knew he had to make a last bid for the summit of completion before the light faded entirely. Muzot then was to be the place where Rilke would find the longed-for peace and stability to complete the series. In February 1922, in a surge of unprecedented creativity, not only did he produce the remaining six *Elegies* but out of them also received the unexpected 'gift' of the *Sonnets to Orpheus*. Less known is the fact that in the same prolific year, he also wrote the revelatory *Brief des jungen Arbeiters* [Letter to a young labourer] and completed his cherished translations of Paul Valéry.

Rilke's relationship with France and French literature strengthened immeasurably during these years at Muzot. On his continuing travels, he increasingly favoured the French-speaking regions of Switzerland, corresponded by letters evermore confidently in French and was producing poems in a language he had not intended as a creative source. This French drive culminated in 1924 when whole suites of poems would be gathered into the collections *Vergers* [Orchards] and *Les Quatrains Valaisans* [The Valaisan quatrains], both published in the months preceding his death at Val-Mont on 19 December 1926. Rilke's long stay in Paris between January and August 1925, which deepened contacts with the French literary world, and finally allowed him to meet and work with his sympathetic translator Maurice Betz, only strengthened this attachment.

II. *Letters around a Garden*

This slender sheaf of twenty-two letters written in French by one of the key European poets of the twentieth century, whose epistolary legacy famously ran to the thousands, might seem just another overlooked fragment of a vast enterprise—a curiosity. Like many of the correspondences Rilke sustained over his working life with highly cultured individuals who believed in the uniqueness of his gift and the immortality of his poetry, this one was with an intelligent, refined young woman from an aristocratic background, Antoinette de Bonstetten. But it is the reason for Rilke's connection with Mlle de Bonstetten that is particularly interesting: namely, the garden of Muzot, the first garden for which he assumed guardianship, entailing not only an obligation to it but also the opportunity to revive its original ordonnance. The modest escarpment plot from which rose Rilke's tower, whose layout he inherited from Raunier, consisted of several long beds dominated by roses and fruit trees, bisected by narrow dirt paths as well as areas of grass and shrubs, giving way beyond the rustic picket fence and stone walls to meadow and vineyard. But over time, elements of the garden had loosed their moorings and all of it had become somewhat disorderly. The tapestry that Rilke imagined had once existed had become unstitched.

Rilke famously possessed a special aesthetic admiration for the rose and readily employed it as a symbol, so much so that like the angel it has almost become a Rilkean trope. But essentially, the rose was for the poet a perennially mysterious still-secretive flower despite its iconic status; the subtle gradations of those closely overlapping petals preoccupied him and the incomparable fragrance, more sensual, nuanced and transcendent than any other flower, drew him irresistibly. Most revealingly, the rose finally provided his self-penned enigmatic epitaph: 'Rose, oh pure contradiction, to be no one's sleep under so many lids.'

The living roses he was now obliged to tend only deepened this passion, for these were *his* roses, not those admired in the gardens or parks of the villas and castles he resided in. With his new responsibility as a gardener managing his own plot, the poet wished to return the Muzot garden to something that better resembled its past as a small Valaisan manor house with box hedges and well-maintained parterres of roses. This was not to create anything pretentious, overly rigid or fussy, but more to take back some control over a garden which had run amok, and, more importantly, resurrect the spirit of the original garden as he imagined it. Once the tower interior was renovated, its historic features meticulously restored and enhanced, Rilke could turn his attention to the exterior. He took an active step in seeking counsel for what in his mind had evolved into a distinct project of design and vegetal reinvigoration. He asked for a recommendation. Enter Mlle de Bonstetten. Antoinette had a keen interest in gardening and was following courses in horticulture at the University of Lausanne. Hers was a name communicated to Rilke as a potential advisor for his garden project and perhaps one who might even lend a practical hand. Once the young lady responded, an exchange of letters commenced, lasting from late March 1924 till late October 1926, only two months before Rilke's death. However, there was a major interruption in the conversation, largely because Rilke spent a significant portion of 1925 in Paris. So in a sense, we have two parts to the correspondence, the brief one of 1924 and the longer one of 1926.

Despite the increasing desire of both parties to meet in person, it took much longer than Rilke had envisaged to finally secure a rendezvous and get down to practical considerations for the Muzot garden. He had written first in the early spring of 1924, expecting a visit from his new consigliere, but fate seemed to be conspiring against them. Rilke ends his first letter of 7 March hopefully: 'And allow me to reiterate in all deference that Muzot awaits you and hopes for you . . . ' (p. 5). His last in June ends on a more beseeching, almost desperate note: 'I am anxious I shall miss you when you return one day via the Loetschberg. Do warn me in good time, I implore you' (p. 26). But in those first letters from 1924, we also find fascinating passages concerning Rilke's reflections on Valéry whose work he had been enthusiastically translating, eloquent evocations of the Muzot tower and its environs, and the experience of living in an old manor house without modern conveniences. But most impressive perhaps are the exquisite, poetically imbued observations of the emergence—or more often reticence—of the Valaisan spring, whose sensitivity and refined perception are surely equal to that of anything Rilke wrote.

With Antoinette de Bonstetten delayed in Geneva, Rilke is obliged to write on through Easter and beyond, lamenting in effortless analogies the difficulties facing plants under the unforgiving Valaisan sun that always serves the monopolizing vine first, the sun that 'commands the flowers brutally' by 'fairly yanking' out the gentle anemones, the sun whose 'impetuous warmth' fools the wisteria or lilies into blooming too early so they 'summon their lovely necklace too precipitously'. In the final letter from 1924, he also writes of his fears for the roses, the diseases and bugs that relentlessly assail them: 'Do there always have to be so many dangers, so many absurd hostilities, so many threats of malignancy in every garden? Were not the gardens of earlier ages with their simple and pious flowers rather less menaced [. . .]?' (p. 25)

It is unclear who recommended the correspondence and when—for who can know if letters from later 1925 have gone astray?—but it seems sensible to assume it was Rilke. Perhaps hoping to rekindle his garden restoration that spring, Rilke writes on 24 February 1926 while convalescing at the clinic of Val Mont above Montreux, confessing how Antoinette had often made incursions into his thoughts during his months in Paris the previous year. Flowers are conscientiously exchanged again and mutually treasured, chosen books too; recommendations of books proffer, all in the customary manner of the poet, and a sense of something beyond a mutual interest in plants and literature lingers evermore compellingly in the space between epistles. On 27 March, with his garden authority travelling in his beloved Provence, Rilke writes a relished evocation of the religious festival at Saintes Marie de la Mer in the Camargue that he once witnessed, leading to a recollection of the lonely atmosphere of old, abandoned cemeteries— lines eerily reminiscent of those by the Belgian symbolist poet Georges Rodenbach (1855–1898): 'And all this

auburn and grey abandon, visited by butterflies and almost
fused with the vegetation of aromatic grasses, forms a great
solar face which perpetually offers to an opulence of forgetting the sum of its hours' (p. 43).

Still installed at Val-Mont, with only sporadic visits to
Muzot, Rilke, in a letter of 15 April, exquisitely expresses
his sorrow at Antoinette departing Morges on lac Léman,
'which, between us, resembles a lovely white page to turn
in order to travel from one text to another' (p. 49). He has
received roses from his correspondent, but more than anything Rilke wishes to be out of the sanatorium and with
her among his own. 'I viewed my rose bushes yesterday and
I so wish you will come soon and discuss them with me, in
their presence, though without forgetting all you had
begun to tell me on the question of "untranslatable music"'
(p. 49). We do not know what Antoinette de Bonstetten
said on the subject of their 'untranslatable music'—nor on
anything else—since her letters have not been recovered.
Thus, while reading the collection, we are obliged merely
to conjure from Rilke's words something of what might
have been in her letters to him. The absence of the cor-
responding letters may seem an impediment, but there are
unforeseen dividends to having only a shadow respondent
whom we see as if through a gauze, her thoughts and

actions indistinct and tantalizingly ambiguous. It makes Antoinette de Bonstetten appear that much more enigmatic and fleeting. The strange atmosphere produced by this one-sidedness serves to better illumine the content of Rilke's letters, to enhance his reflections, to make more tender his yearning and to frame some of his finest lines. Her fugacious presence also tends to magnify Rilke's air of vulnerability as his health declines. In some way, the absence of her letters obligates the reader to garner every fibre of nourishment from his; the sacrifice of her own reality, the concealment of her actual words, means Rilke's voice alone is responsible for presence.

It seems that Rilke had already instigated changes to the garden through de Bonstetten's advice, but he still longed for her to grace his rose beds with a personal inspection and recommendations for improvement. Thus, on 19 April, he writes: 'Ah, come, dear Mademoiselle, lend my flowers some ideas. It has always seemed to me that they ponder the void through lack of education' (p. 52). Then in May, he was left in suspense no longer. Rilke, with his doctor's tacit agreement, took leave from Val-Mont to meet de Bonstetten in Sierre. Later they ascended the winding road to Veyras, then took the narrow dirt lane to Muzot. Now they finally stood in the garden together discussing

plans. On 27 May, a buoyed-up Rilke writes to his friend
and confidant Nanny Wunderly-Volkart:

> Last Friday I was in Sierre with Mlle de Bonstetten:
> it was marvellous to look over the garden with
> someone who has such a deep knowledge of
> this subject, suddenly all is transformed! We have
> drawn up the final project for restoration and sim-
> plification of the garden scheduled for the end of
> October. A long parterre of roses, *unified* (we have
> to make changes due to the ever-encroaching shade
> of the chestnuts!) and this *edged with box. Box*
> everywhere in fact, replacing the stones. A scatter-
> ing of bushes here and there. Not much else, but
> above all some organization, a little order! How
> long I have had to wait for such counsel: this school
> of hers in Neuchâtel seems perfect—it will furnish
> everything and at a very fair price.[4]

The letters between Rilke and de Bonstetten spanned
the period of his increasing ill health. Like others written at
that time from Muzot, Val-Mont or the Hotel Bellevue, the
letters provided Rilke with an indispensable companionship

---

4 Rainer Maria Rilke, *Briefe an Nanny Wunderly-Volkart, Band II*
[Letters to Nanny Wunderly-Volkart, VOL. 2] (Frankfurt am Main: Insel
Verlag, 1977), p. 1136.

and spiritual underlay during the last, difficult phase of his life when he was unable to travel any great distance and the monotony of the invalid's unchanging days set in. In certain passages of these letters, Rilke reveals his exasperation as he acknowledges that the body, which generally served him well despite his sensitivity and fragility, had at this point almost betrayingly broken its longstanding harmony with his mind and spirit—a sharp contrast with the past when the body's accord with mind and spirit had fostered creative growth. Rilke writes in a letter of early May: 'a malevolent magic (one of those tiny errors which gradually lead to huge deviations) has, so to speak, lead me into the enemy camp' (p. 64)—and later of a 'discordance' between his mind and body. This breakdown in the traditional order of a hard-won physiological equipoise aggravated his despondency.

However, friendship and its careful amplification proved a counterbalance to this new reality. The propitious nature of the relationship that evolved between the increasingly fragile poet and the young student of horticulture, to which these twenty-two letters testify, tempered the encroaching isolation of Rilke's circumstance. And the Muzot garden was transformed at the eleventh hour through de Bonstetten's direct influence, just as Rilke had intended. For hadn't he explained to her in the letter of 19 April: 'Before a house massive and severe as a canon of the Middle Ages, the garden really must extend like the opened pages of a beautiful illuminated antiphony. It must dare over five lines to propose a precise music' (p. 52)? Antoinette de Bonstetten's verve and knowledge, no less her fateful presence, had helped configure the leaves of those illuminations, to set in train a more harmonious arrangement of notes.

Will Stone

1924

LETTER 1

Château de Muzot-sur-Sierre

Valais (Suisse)

7th March 1924

Dear Mademoiselle,

What joy it brings me to know that the other day
I chanced to obey the interior voice which
suddenly commanded me not to delay in sending
my parcel to you: thus it was able to join you at a
most favourable reposeful moment for reading.
Thank you for the great welcome you have given
to these books—and that you wished to mark
their arrival in such moving words to me. Since I
never look at reviews of my work, I remain singularly capable of drawing any authentic benedic-
tion from a scattering of consenting voices which
come through to me from time to time, and I

3

would certainly never confuse the accent of your own.

If you had come to Caux towards the end of January, it would have been easy for me to pay you a little visit. For this winter the penurious state of my health had obliged me to take refuge at Val-Mont. I returned to Muzot so little rehabilitated that it is more than likely that in a few weeks' time I shall return to the sanatorium of Dr Widmer[1] for another round of treatment. The sole thing that can console me in this grim necessity . . . (and which for me is rather exceptional, since I have lived for the last twenty years in perfect accord with my nature, never having recourse to a doctor) the only consolation would be to know that you were close by and to be able to profit from this neighbourliness, to forget in your company the disagreeable reason for my inadvertent displacement. But I am most fearful that you will not stay on so long, and in another sense I had always clung to the hope that I could better support myself with the coming of spring.

I wish you a gentle time of rest—and that your sojourn in the mountains will be blessed by the sun and all those welcome influences which perform without our knowledge, and all under the guise of that good feeling of tiredness.

And allow me to reiterate in all deference that Muzot awaits you and hopes for you!

Rainer Maria Rilke

1 The clinic of Val-Mont, or Valmont as it appears today, dramatically perched above Montreux on lac Léman, was designed by the architect Henri Verrey and established in 1905 by the innovative Dr Henri August Widmer. Then, as now, it specialized in mental illnesses and nervous, nutritional, and digestive disorders.

LETTER 2

Muzot-sur-Sierre
Valais (Suisse)
26th March 2024

Dear Mademoiselle,

Despite the generous sun of the last fortnight,
the Valais spring is tardy in arriving this year.
Here are the first anemones that I gathered from
our hills—how charming they are, don't you
think? And they speak so well of the season's
risks, having clad themselves, in spite of their confidence, in this tiny silvery fur which makes them
almost unrecognizable in the greyness of the
stony and still-bare earth.

Thank you kindly for your letter of March
15th; how good it is that you could return to
your work so fully rested. As for Geneva, I was

there for long enough and over a good number of visits to endorse all you say: that it is a truly 'exceptional' city. Greet it warmly on the part of your most devoted

R. M. Rilke

Château de Muzot-sur-Sierre

Valais (Suisse)

1ˢᵗ April 1924

Dear Mademoiselle,

I am comforted to know that these humble anemones should invite you to confirm the arrival of spring in the countryside around Geneva . . . but how much more assured it appears than our own and how much more 'sung'. You heard the first larks! Here, after a few trial runs without much to follow from the blackbirds and tits, we have reverted to the low mass, and it's only the spade now that speaks drily, preparing the future vintage amid the hard and bare vines. And the earth responds with the silence of an ill-awoken church. You see those chilly anemones that opened prematurely and a few devout primroses, modest in stature and poorly clad? They are the little morning mass of the Valaisan spring. It lacks those soft rains which elsewhere usher in a forgotten caress, falling in long lines like a fluid script, a loving correspondence between sky and earth where so many promises of the future pour forth. Here, when the sky is obscured, the breath of snow which comes down the mountains immediately expunges any aspirations the rain may have had. It rains awkwardly, and the sky inscribes these few lines in the air, without pleasure, like a schoolchild with fingers frozen stiff. And a few days later when the sun reappears, it commands the flowers brutally, fairly yanking them out from the earth by their hair, scarcely flattering them. It overwhelms with its impetuous warmth which they cannot properly comprehend. It levers open the chestnuts, but quickly, rifling through them without tenderness; and then one day it abruptly commands that the wisteria should come into bloom, and on another day the lilacs—wisteria and lilacs both hasten to obey and summon their lovely necklace too precipitously. You might say it is the vine alone that this Valais sun addresses with a measure of politeness and respect. Only for her does it permit a lingering slowness; for the sun's true calling here is to labour over and bring to fruition the vine—all the other plants it views as so many amateurs, dilettantes, and mistreats them often. Later, as all around, the waters also run only to the vine, and it is a strenuous task to persuade it that in such an arid landscape, other thirsts exist beyond its own.

You see, there is great austerity in this old valley of the Rhone, and this old Muzot, which has known seven centuries, seems proud to partake in austere traditions. More than this, my life is that of a recluse, and a captive for the greater part of the year. Even in a land less severe, an old tower like this will hold firm: in the Valais (as in Spain, a country which resembles this landscape), the walls of an old farmstead still have more strength; the whole atmosphere and even the light seem to prove them right. It is indescribable how such a dwelling subjugates you, leaving you only the freedom you can find in your heart or in

your thoughts, but, on the other hand, it serves
to illuminate the countryside for you and even
the space: for these ancient towers were not
placed by chance—they are arranged like the
pawns in a most noble game of chess, one con-
stellated towards all the others, and God knows
if, after long, meditative intervals, this game only
goes on to end in some final victory, in which this
being of all slowness will rejoice, the one who
with eternal wisdom knows how to move the
pawns of the centuries.

This reclusion, this complete silence which I
endure, and which turn by turn protects me
through the long winter months, softens a little
towards Easter; Muzot, soon after I discovered it,
and retained all my meagre strength, was pur-
chased by a friend of mine from Winterthur,[1] this
generous friend, who, so taken up with his own
affairs and never one to stay long, now tends to
make an all-too-brief appearance in his Valaisan
property and will bring one of his friends along
with him. Usually, it's his arrival which sets in
train a series of visits, for now my friends often
choose to make a stop in Sierre, whether on their

return from Italy or on a quick stopover to enjoy a few hours of conversation in which I initially engage with some surprise, dulled by such a long and laborious silence. For the most part, I put these friends up in the Bellevue[2]—for Muzot only provides a modest attic room in its gable for the most forgiving amongst them, and in any case this guest room is only habitable in the warmer months. From the Hotel Bellevue, which is close to the Sierre train station, one may climb in around half an hour to my tower, located on the north-east side of the valley, up this slope which, since the most ancient times, bears the name Noble-Contrée.[3] Despite the short distance, one can't make out Muzot from Sierre, my tower remains hidden by another hill close to which there are a few modern buildings scattered on the site of a ruined manor house. But once arrived in the hamlet of Veyras, where the lane makes a turn, you suddenly have the ancient tower there before you, and this fine solitary poplar which announces it like a herald at arms.

That I had not written this letter to you a year earlier! What might have come to pass then

fills me with the most profound regret: that you
could have come by Sierre or even stayed at Sion
without even having to attempt this undemand-
ing little climb. You love to listen—well, a letter
does not properly speak! (And in any case, in
writing this one, I must confess I was suffering
rather and indisposed, thus I fear it will only
respond imperfectly.) But we will fare better, the
country and myself, when one day you come
here, 'to listen'.

To you, in all deference

RM Rilke

1 Rilke's patron, Swiss merchant and philanthropist Werner
Reinhart (1884–1951).

2 The Hotel Bellevue in Sierre; since 1967 it has served as the
town hall.

3 Literally 'noble land', the name given to the collection of
traditionally wine producing villages such as Veyras and
Miège in the immediate environs of Muzot.

Château de Muzot-sur-Sierre
Valais (Suisse)
4th April 1924

Dear Mademoiselle,

They alerted me that Paul Valéry, admirable poet,
would appear tomorrow, Saturday, at five o'clock
in the afternoon at the Athenaeum in Geneva for
a conference on Baudelaire: the idea struck me
that this conference, prepared rather hastily,
might not be widely circulated and thus had perhaps escaped your notice; I have an ardent desire
to be in attendance but I am still not in the best of
shape—besides, Valéry was thoughtful to let me
know that he will more than likely make a stop at
Sierre, next Sunday, to spend a few hours with
me, so I have decided to wait for him here! But I
wanted to let you know about his appearance.

For, amongst my contemporaries, it is his work which I admire above all others'; I spent the winter before last translating him—which for me was a joyful and eternally evocative labour.

This poet, sure in himself, kept silent for almost a quarter century; he only picked up his work of art again around 1917 to produce definitively great books, one after the other. This brought him a certain degree of renown without him yet being fully appreciated in the wider world; also his work does not lack a certain difficulty, yet it resists being hermetic. Its abundant beauty gives of itself to whoever persists there.

In the event that none of his works have as yet fallen into your hands, I am copying you (back to front) a little poem amongst those I attempted to translate. This sample will give you a better idea of his gift than anything I could rashly propose.[1]

What a shame that Geneva can't be a little nearer; and yet this letter will still find you this evening, I very much hope!

1 Rilke refers to the poem 'Les Grenades' which appeared in *Charmes*, published in 1922.

Chateau de Muzot-sur-Sierre

Valais (Suisse)

12th April 1924, Saturday

Dear Mademoiselle,

. . . 'something of a disappointment . . .'? How
this extraordinary man, having obeyed that other
goddess, has in effect perhaps made a return to
the 'glorious intelligence'. It's not by chance that
in his youth, in his initial desire to fix a point in
the space of the spirit, he settled on Leonardo da
Vinci, who, likewise only saw in art one of
multiple possibilities to practice in the funda-
mental. If we return to laws, emotivity probably
appears something accidental, and we hardly seek
to exhibit it, nor even to evoke it. As for 'the

invisible', it culminates nevertheless by arising from our conversations which were always rather rushed, given the brevity of time, but still inexhaustible. Late in the evening, the vision of a dialogue which must surely one day follow the *Eupalinos*[1] was confided to me, and there, I assure you, the sublime poet who dwells discreetly in Valéry could no longer remain concealed. Incidentally, during the afternoon and evening, and then again the other morning, which permitted us a few more moments in commune before departure—how many aspects so varied and almost irreconcilable one to another had I remarked! It was this which preoccupied me and amazed me most through these last years: those changes of expression within the same being, which transformed him from one moment to the next, either they seemed to tear him from himself or, so to speak, restore him to his equilibrium . . . ; with the majority of people the play of these incessant transformations has something disconcerting about it; rarely do we divine in them that interior continuity (searched

for by Marcel Proust) of which these are the last
waves; rarely do we have the good fortune or the
acumen to try out a synthesis of the kind which
speaks to you. Each of us present ourselves as a
collective being whose innumerable elements are
in a constant state of regrouping, renewing or
dying, supporting one another or at variance
with one another, turn by turn. In a world so rich
and so mobile where almost never does one
moment explain that which follows, altruism is
not a simple thing: for to whom is it addressed?
It's certain, by the way, at the base of all impulse
towards others, there lies a profound discomfort
as regards ourselves, or rather a secret despair to
bear ourselves. But that, I feel, in no way dimin-
ishes this momentum, which, on the contrary,
becomes more human. Imagine! We abandon
ourselves in order to approach that unknown
other, who in their way also take leave of themselves; and we hope in some vague manner to
understand the other that we see only from the
outside, for they are this distinct being of whose
difficulties we remain ignorant (and because,

perhaps, it will help us to arrive at a clearer understanding of ourselves). The other is nothing more than a detour towards ourselves. It's already so much if from this calamity of supporting oneself is born the need to rescue others, instead of making them suffer (as, for example, does Tolstoy).

We need art (and still!) or all the resources and expectations of childhood, and the constant contribution of so many things to support ourselves, alone. A willing house; a garden innocent and giving; the curve of birds in the air; the winds, the rains, memories and the calm of a starry firmament stretching to the infinite: all this just so a human being can settle with his heart!

One day you must tell me about this Gwatt[2] which was part of your childhood; I have a sense of it, I am beginning to form in my mind its almost languid abandon where inexpressible influences perpetuate . . .

Yes, I like to write in French, though I have never managed to *write* this language (which more than any other compels perfection since it

permits it) without error and even without insidi-
ous transgressions. A large part of my correspondence is written in French. I thought, in this way,
to remove the other language from virtually all
use save for art and to make of it the pure matter
of my verbal employ. I managed this for quite
some time, then suddenly, this winter, French
began to encroach on the very terrain it was
meant to protect. A little in spite of myself, I
ended up filling an entire notebook with French
'verse', works which you understand are not
wholly irreproachable.

Unfortunately, to say all, one must know all
languages. I recollect that one of the first reasons
for forming a poem in French was the absence of
any equivalent to the delectable word: *Verger* . . .

In the past, when I was focused on Russian,
I recall having to combat other, even graver
jealousies.

A fresh lingering snow has just nipped spring
in the bud; one senses it with disheartenment and
impatience. How this untimely whiteness pains
the eyes. I am most fearful that in Geneva, you

will have experienced the same sudden setback, but I wish you a Sunday which allows you to keep it from your mind one way or another!

R. M. Rilke

1 Paul Valéry's *Eupalinos, or the Architect* was first published by *La Nouvelle Revue Française* in 1923.
2 Gwatt is a district of the lakeside town of Thun in the Bernese Oberland where the Bonstetten family had settled.

LETTER 6

Muzot-sur-Sierre

Good Friday, Easter 1924

Dear Mademoiselle,

Muzot has already entered the season of guests
(despite the earth which quivers though spring is
turned back from us once more by distracted and
malign winds). Aside from a few tulips, my little
garden has not yet recited its Easter prayer; I
would have preferred it to be the one to wish you
a happy Eastertide, but since it is unable, I hereby
offer you another blossoming that anyway you
already know; only its obedient reflection is
added to my spirit.[1] It's worth remembering that
if I was able to offer its reflection, it was only
because it had rendered me clear as crystal.

Rilke

1 Rilke attached his translation of Valéry's poem 'Palme' to
the letter, with the French text beside it.

Château de Muzot-sur-Sierre
11th June 1924

Dear Mademoiselle,

If your successive occupations, that of caring for the sick and caring for flowers, were not likely to have accustomed you to a long and indulgent patience, I should fear to have been reported 'missing', after a far-too-prolonged epistolary absence . . . To explain it, I would be tempted to enumerate the numberless visits I have had since Easter; their following on from one another forming an almost uninterrupted chain—and to be among these friends I was obliged to desert my desk. It's true that I did find moments here and there to write something, but the unremitting employ of the living word (and how much more preferable to that which we write) utterly spoiled me in service of the pen.

However, I have thought of you often, and sometimes such thoughts are mixed with a little hope of hearing an announcement of your passage through Sierre . . . Your last letter was precisely one of those that evoke other questions instead of dictating responses; we should have spoken from one side to the other. It's only now that a book André Gide has just sent me (*Incidences*)[1] has clarified what you were saying about the Valéry conference. Gide says somewhere: 'Criticism is the basis of all art'. Doubtless it is this critique that Valéry has undertaken in supposing a 'Baudelaire recipe'; for if it is an accomplished pleasure to discover the same 'recipe', in a work of art, this pleasure would appear even more sublime in that it is free; and having never been used, it will be employed all the less to do something else after having been expressed. Formulated, this recipe becomes as never before a recipe of luxury, useless and imaginary, and through its subtle invention, almost congenial to the work of art itself. If I understand rightly, it's more his perfect desire to eliminate chance which leads Valéry to establish supposed intentions, possible and at the same time impossible by their very expression; for if every work arranges itself by obeying a latent law, that law remains inexpressible while it is acting; and what one discovers afterwards is merely a foster sister of that law with which we amuse ourselves in admitting that it might have served.

It is nature which produces with more simplicity, for, in spite of all, she is more shielded from our discoveries and our curiosity which pursues her without ever reaching her inexhaustible secret. I send you a few samples of the best my garden has to offer at present. Almost every day I spend a little time amongst my roses, to fight for them, they whose spines are of no practical use against the most fearsome enemies. Do there always have to be so many dangers, so many absurd hostilities, so many threats of malignancy in every garden? Were not the gardens of earlier ages with their simple and pious flowers rather less menaced, before chemistry was mixed in with them . . . ? Mine sometimes appears to me a veritable hospice of flowers—if you do come by, you will surely have no recourse to depart from your present vocation amongst the invalids.

Perhaps very soon, by the way, I will make out in the distance the gable of Bellerive;[2] I promised last year that I would return for the horse show in Thun—which is already the 14th and 15th of this month. And you, dear Mademoiselle, will you stay on in Geneva with no further holidays for the rest of the summer? I am anxious I shall miss you when you return one day via the Loetschberg.[3] Do warn me in good time, I implore you.

R.M. Rilke

1 Gide's *Incidences* constitutes a collection of shorter prose and was first published by Gallimard in May 1924.

2 Rilke refers to the striking roof of Bellerive, a landmark building in Gwatt.

3 The Loetschberg is a long rail tunnel beneath the Bernese Alps that connects the Valais to the Bernese Oberland and the Thunersee. Its construction began in 1907, and after several disasters, regular services finally commenced in 1913. It is still the only direct route for travellers moving between these two regions by car or passenger train.

1926

Rilke in a lane near Muzot, undated, source unknown.

LETTER 8

Val-Mont by Glion

Vaud (Suisse)

24th February 1926

Dear Mademoiselle,

Last year, during the long months that I passed in
Paris, I was often aware of the interruption to our
epistolary relations, discovering in myself a spon-
taneous need to communicate to you such and
such impression amongst the countless with
which Paris had filled me. Moreover, I have been
wanting to write to you since my return to
Muzot . . . but the state of my health, which has
never been robust over these past years, has since
upset, along with all my other projects, my correspondence. For the third time, abandoning my
old Valais tower, I was obliged to seek refuge at
Val-Mont; and it's from here that I dare to
address these few lines at random, ignorant of

29

whether you are even still in Geneva. It is not
beyond the realms of possibility that I could
make a trip there, for a few days, in the spring . . .
having missed you several times at Vuippens,[1] I
would be overjoyed to meet you just the once.
Admittedly, I would have far preferred to receive
you in my Muzot tower: but will you ever make it
there? I don't know what intuition led me to
signal my presence at Val-Mont to you, I was
going to say: my dispiriting isolation which is
consoled by only a handful of books, but even
books, if one reads them in a prison, leave you
with a singular desire for movement and evasion,
suggesting so many possible situations which in
no way correspond with the monotonous
neutrality which is the lot of the poor reader.
The idea came to me, without any clear reason,
that perhaps you would pass one day by
Montreux or Territet,[2] on your way to or from
Geneva. Know, dear Mademoiselle, in the case of
this implausible notion, you would bring infinite
consolation to one Val-Mont detainee and,
ascending by Glion, do charity by paying him
a brief visit. I believe that I would never have
risked the temerity of such an idea if you had not

chosen the vocation of active charity. My provisory situation brings me vaguely closer to those who are in need. It's under this title that I recall myself to your good memory of yesteryear.

Believe, dear Mademoiselle, in my continuing devotion.

R. M. Rilke

P.S. I saw M. Schneeli[3] on a number of occasions in Paris; for Vuippens, I returned to Switzerland too late last year, to run into him again there!

1 Vuippens is an ancient municipality in the canton of Fribourg.

2 Territet is the lakeside village adjoining Montreux on its south side which is linked to Glion above it (Glion-sur-Territet) by a famous funicular railway which dates from 1883.

3 Rilke refers to Dr Gustav Schneeli (1872–1944) who lived at the castle of Vuippens. Schneeli studied art history with Jakob Burckhardt in Basel and later became a painter influenced by impressionism and symbolism, residing in Rome, Paris, and Munich before finally settling at Vuippens after the outbreak of the First World War.

LETTER 9

Val-Mont by Glion
6th March 1926

Dear Mademoiselle,

The 'flowers' that you wrote to me have admir-
ably tolerated the long journey, for why, since you
mention them, wait for others and not resolutely
call flowers these lines so fresh, so immediate in
their quick blooming, so filled with the sap of
events in which you have participated, and your
memories!

As for Paris (no: I was no longer there during
the month of October), the places you fre-
quented are those very same which have always
been dearest to me, the most familiar, with in
addition—though you didn't actually name it—
the Ile Saint-Louis; I am not surprised by the

wonder you felt there! Quite the contrary. My
protracted experience in earlier times invests me
with the authority to find eternally justified this
happy surprise which was yours. As for myself,
being less young, how many times, through those
long months of last year, had I ruled in favour of
all my old influences; some days I even found
insufficient: experiencing who knows what
need for a fuller consent, a still-more-active
admiration . . . The miracle of this city has no
equal anywhere, this city which, vast and seething
with all utilitarian and urban ambitions, has not
only known how to remain a landscape, one of
the most authentic landscapes in the world—but
has never lost the attendant grace of its immense
sky. All the great cities I know have somehow
managed to weaken and dispirit theirs. Whilst
Paris . . . I wonder if the uncountable life of this
capital has not in some way added to the freedom
of its space an element of ecstasy? Paris knew how
to win over, to delight its sky. This ornamental
pond of the Luxembourg, so vast, so finely pro-
portioned that it sometimes appears lacklustre
and restrained (like so many expanses of water

in gardens open to the public), that lack this generosity of airy space which lends this lovely mirror an infinitude of limpid and ever-changing abundance!

And what distance (don't you think?) so *paysagiste*[1] which spreads between the little abandoned garden of Saint-Julien-le-Pauvre and Notre-Dame de Paris . . . ! We must believe that you were expertly guided to have discovered it, this charming patch of greenery and decay, unknown to so many Parisians, of whose charm we were perhaps the last to have been aware, menaced as it is by developers. Just imagine that I had been unaware of it myself right up until my last stay. In the past, often stopping by Saint-Julien-le-Pauvre, even for the services of Armenian worship, I had never dared approach the little lateral door of the sanctuary. Some friends encouraged me to, and ever since, I have spent many a summer afternoon in this enclosure whose ambience like that of a dream draws you away from all that was preoccupying your mind in the instant before. For me it was like the late discovery between two pages joined to one another, an unknown image in a book already read and leafed through; surprise which not only established itself in the present, but which I would have liked, through a tender ruse of the soul, to replace in a past where it was surely missing.

1 Painter of landscapes.

Val-Mont by Glion-sur-Territet

Vaud (Suisse)

20th March 1926

Dear Mademoiselle,

It would not be enough to say that these other
flowers (after the written ones) had arrived fresh:
they arrived perfectly rested, cheerful! What's
more, you tucked them up so well in their
triple-travel bed! These three layers, these three
regions . . . , I could say, these three strophes of
flowers which were represented like three degrees
of rustic intimacy, and which, in their ensemble,
were setting out like a distant and secret mythol-
ogy of the eternal promenade. Woodland
blooms, little anemones of the meadow, freesias
of gardens, and the lone svelte tulip, so young, a
little conceited (and so apart, so apart from the

hundreds of tulips which overstate themselves in the florists of Montreux). I am at a loss to name the red flowers, with the green calyx, but it seems to me that I encountered them somewhere in the past, and in observing them attentively, memories welled up from the distance to provide some explanation. What I recognize, above all, are these delicate anemones that I was going to wake up in my large garden in Rome; for they slept on when I was leaving, in the morning, and it was I who threw them the temperament of the day between their hesitant eyelids; but it was then they who, afterwards, so much surpassed me in rejecting their tender petals, seized by some receptive ardour, opening to the sun to such an extent that sometimes they lacked the strength to close again at nightfall. And yesterday evening, the dear ones, after I had cut the stems, made themselves comfortable in a little glass, and deceived right away by the insistence of the electric light, they set themselves to repeat this gesture of welcome and abandon of which I had always thought was in some measure that of Saint-Thérèse, as imagined by Bernini or Rodin. So many years later, I sang

it, this unforgettable movement of a feeble spring-
time calyx in the *Sonnets to Orpheus*:

> floral muscle, that of the anemone
> meadow morning gradually opened up,
> down to her lap the polyphonic
> light pours out of the loud sky,
>
> in the silent flower star more tense
> muscle of infinite reception,
> sometimes with abundance so overwhelmed,
> that the angel of downfall
>
> scarce capable of the far-rebounded
> to bring back leaf boundaries to you:
> you, resolve and strength of how many worlds![1]

. . . .

(the little flowers before me, do they doubt that I
recite the song of their modest glory which so far
surpasses us?)

But of these strophes, mine, I come back to
those of your mail. Had there been a fourth layer
the sonnet would be perfect; but, no, it wants for
nothing, whilst the ultimate tercet was formed
under the very action of opening the package, and

its subject would be the successive discovery of these three layers and the rhythm of your walk. That the happy country was there! I have since looked for Saint-Cyr[2] on the map; the imagination, the memory, the nostalgia guided me there, seeing those names, one more charming than the next, I could have thought myself mistaken, and to have strayed onto a celestial sphere, amongst the constellations. You are, by the way, very close to Aix, a country I know well and once thought to set down roots. My God, you are no longer at the Amandiers,[3] and I do not decipher so well the new spring faith that you have chosen in: Les Lecques?[4] I hope that this finds you there, with all my grateful joy, before your departure.

R. M. Rilke

1 Translation of 'Sonnet 5' from Book II by the translator.

2 Rilke refers to Saint Cyr-sur-Mer on the Cote d'Azur.

3 'Amandiers' probably refers to a hotel in Saint Cyr-sur-Mer.

4 'Les Lecques' refers to the adjoining coastal hamlet of Saint Cyr-les-Lecques.

LETTER 11

Dear Mademoiselle,

Having read your letter, instead of searching for some way of making your return to the 'German mindset' less onerous, I should rather implore you: Stay! Prolong! April 15th is too close! Stay at least till the 25th of May, and if it is absolutely necessary to return, bring these days in Provence to a close with a pilgrimage to Saintes-Maries-de-la-Mer (25th May) of which I could not speak to you in a single letter without greatly exceeding the proportions of the epistolary. This double pilgrimage (double, for it attracts not only the country devotees of the two 'Marie', but also a large number of Spanish 'gitanos', who in impassioned opposition hastily converge to worship, not the two saints reunited in a twin shrine with a double canopy, which for hours, suspended over their little roost above the altar, they lower down, with the slowness of centuries, above the crowd straining towards the miracle . . . , but their black servant, Sainte Sarah. Just imagine this double game of devotion, the extreme tension and how all these sounds, songs with Provençal vocalizations collide with the stormy basses of 'Vive Sainte Sarah!', hurled against the angels . . .) But here my parentheses have devoured my first phrase; I won't reclaim it. I will just tell you that we stayed in that high, fortified church with its battlements, built in the reign of King René, a whole day and a whole night; and tearing ourselves away finally from this melodious drama, half-planned, half-improvised and to which we had only been mere spectators, we encountered on exiting the vast morning sea assailing that expanse of Camargue and the lovely youthfulness of a wind on that the day of celebration!

And so ended one of my stays in Provence, in that Provence that I have never left without the tacit promise of returning to spend a part of my life there (as if it could contain so many different chapters!). But above all my memories I could place as epigraph your two lines:

'And we recognize, with beating heart, the house of our dreams' . . .

May God bless your pharmacist who, with these few pills from a condensed past, knows how to invent such a perfect cure for the future.[1] Your 'competition' ended up as something touching for him; no doubt you shall accept him as a collaborator for this celebrated museum of the future. I promise to be amongst your first visitors and to show myself worthy of the importance of these excavations. I will stop there, I swear! Before every glass case, and I will not hesitate to kneel to unveil those objects which prove difficult to discern. It is possible, however, that from time to time I will chance a look towards the courtyard . . . (Might your occupations permit you to meet me there?) for, to be honest, it is the courtyards of museums in Provence and in Spain which always drew me most. Cemeteries without bodies where just a few stones signify death, carved in places or worn away, who knows—

others adorned with that proud Roman script
which seems to have been formed to deify the
words and to learn to read them across centuries.
And all this auburn and grey abandon, visited by
butterflies and almost fused with the vegetation
of aromatic grasses, forms a great solar face which
perpetually offers to an opulence of forgetting
the sum of its hours. In such places can it be said
that we are drawn to linger? . . . We can go on
there. Unoccupied, and at the same moment
replete, we discover in ourselves a slow permanence of the heart, protected from acquisitions
and losses. How I yearn to return there!

I would so much like to contribute to your
little 'regional' library, but I haven't come across
by chance anything quite suitable on my fur-
nished shelves, apart from this issue of the
Mercure [2] in which M. Alexandre Arnoux evokes
a Provençal land quite distant from yours; but
(how not to be touched by this coincidence) he
speaks there of a curious custodian of the
museum . . . and, amongst other things, of these
'black stars' [3] that I for one have never observed
and of which perhaps your pharmacist possesses
some rare specimen.

The spring of Muzot? It is not yet with us; and once under way, everything has already moved on past it. This famous sun of the wine growers thinks only of the resistant feet of the vine. As for the flowers, it almost yanks them out by tempting them, you might say it performs its labours (do excuse the image) with a corkscrew. Thus, even the Valais spring is imploring you: Stay! Stay!

R. M. Rilke

1 The pharmacist of Saint-Cyr-sur-Mer had discovered Roman mosaics on the hillside.

2 *Mercure de France* was originally a French gazette dating from the seventeenth century, which was reborn at the end of the nineteenth century as a literary review and publisher concerned with the symbolist movement. The magazine closed in 1965, but the publishing house survived and was absorbed by Gallimard.

3 The only references to 'black stars' in horticulture are the gladiolus 'black star' or sword lily, a modern cultivar, and the 'black star snake plant' (*Sansevieria dracaena*), a house plant native to West Africa.

Easter Sunday 1926

Dear Mademoiselle,

Is it, is it really possible! And I who continue to conceive these little Provençal plans for you; it's true that you have (invited to this sudden decision) concentrated the juice of ripened farewells and made more arduous the beautiful and sorrowful face of departure. And why would you not, at the same time, have obliged the honour of destiny to arrange for you a happy return!

For my part, how could I not be happy to know that you are in Morges, whilst you haven't forgotten my need for charity, which has scarcely lessened since I confided it to you. What has diminished is my fear of having forever dishonoured the joy of a meeting by this overlong silence prior to our recent correspondence. Did you at least note the happy influence of your messages upon this isolated being at one of these crossroads whose secret highway of life seems so alluring?

The beautiful consolation is that the great cross-roads take on the form of a star; one must be able to contemplate them from a great height to properly perceive them.

If it's still the 'sister' to whom I address myself, that she reminds Mademoiselle de Bonstetten (whom you judge 'timid') my most ancient hopes of meeting her, which date from the day when she wished to take interest in (on the instigation of a friend of hers) the fate of a stranger eager for a miracle; this unknown had no desire to leave Switzerland, and Mademoiselle Antoinette de Bonstetten had (as she will recall) a most charming indulgence for this obstinacy. Was there in this vague hope of being able to stay in this hospitable country some presentiment of the realization of Muzot? It's possible. Everything fits. And those things which do not come to fruition as long as the temporary failure rests in safe hands form the foundations of future accomplishments. In this time, with what prudent pen (the only way to sketch a vain and virtual gratitude) have I inscribed the name of Mademoiselle de Bonstetten in my address book!

May it therefore be granted to me to inaugurate such a hallowed feeling . . .

Unable to move from here, I remain ignorant of the convenience of correspondence between Morges and Montreux (or Territet). If the trains find themselves ill-disposed for the return, would you have the kindness to arrange a meeting in the location which is most attainable to you? The doctor permits me a measure of freedom and I see that he is pleased if I am able to profit from it a little; it's almost a form of obedience to him if you force me to neglect awhile the too-regular dictation of my treatments. In saying that, I become timid also, for am I even capable of offering myself up to your attentive generosity? These last days were flooded with illness; I felt more ailing, devalued as a two-penny bit to which one should make known that, in these hurriedly passing times, it is no longer quite enough to amount to the least bouquet of violets!

R. M. Rilke

Val-Mont by Glion

15th April 1926

Dear Mademoiselle,

Since 'our' Friday, I made, one after the other,
two little trips, one to Lausanne and another,
yesterday, to Muzot and I returned here in the
end fatigued and downcast; for even this fatigue
makes me realize that finally exiting from my
seclusion, I am hardly capable of serious labours!
But I set myself the task of writing to the
Grand-Hôtel at Saint-Cyr. Your light-footed
pen, amiable, sought to move ahead of my own:
your letter, which arrived yesterday, instructs
me, whilst renewing somehow our conversation,
which was clearly only interrupted by the arbi-
trary dictation of the one hour by train. You tell

me that it was of some two and a half hours'
duration: now, I find that if we are getting into
figures, of a perfect insufficiency which has no
need to be proven. Also, I was saddened to learn
that, already tomorrow, you will take leave
of Morges and that lake which, between us,
resembles a lovely white page to turn in order to
travel from one text to another.

I remain with your beautiful roses, awaiting
the moment which allows me to write to you
more fully at Sinneringen.[1]

I viewed my rose bushes yesterday and I so
wish you will come soon and discuss them with
me, in their presence, though without forgetting
all you had begun to tell me on the question of
'untranslatable music'.

And as to last Friday and to all the 'future
Fridays', it will always be for me to say 'Thank
you', unless I deem it more expressive to remain
silent.

R. M. Rilke

My little package from Easter (a book, charming in part, by this poor Louis Codet,[2] might it follow you and meet you somewhere). Doubtless you have made a stop en route, but where? Aix? (I do hope so!)

1 The castle at Sinneringen in the canton of Bern was built in 1729 and acquired by Johann Karl von Bonstetten in 1800. After the estate was sold out of the family in 1889, the von Bonstetten family rebought the property in 1922, finally selling it to the Lüthi family in 1925.

2 Louis Codet (1876–1914) was a French writer who collaborated on the first issue of *La Nouvelle Revue Française*. He died in Le Havre after injuries sustained while serving in Steenstrate, Flanders in November 1914.

LETTER 14

Never have I had to collaborate in destroying a family home (one after another, they had all disappeared before my time, the last on the death of my great-grandfather); but the simple conscience which, in me, affirms their legendary existence makes me singularly able to share in the sorrow of your current occupation. To survive the life of certain things, to tell oneself that from now on, they will remain ignored, worse, unknown, that they will renounce themselves to the extent that they become saints, accomplishing the same act in human terms and not even being able to promise their paradise which dwelled within us . . .

Monday

. . . but Muzot is coming on now, I feel it, a new
era with its garden reorganized, when I say organ-
ized I mean put in some kind of order for the first
time. Thanks to you, these few vague parterres
have reconfigured themselves, as Valéry might
have it, and have become conscious of the house
for which they will be the flyleaf. And their order
will in turn influence that of the house, which has
become rather drab and morose first beneath the
darkening of its occupant and second through his
extended absence. Before a house massive and
severe as a canon of the Middle Ages, the garden
really must extend like the opened pages of a
beautiful illuminated antiphony. It must dare over
five lines to propose a precise music. Until now,
from my poor disorientated terrace only scattered
notes have emanated, where the melody only
makes itself known by the caprice of indifferent
and distracted chance. Ah, come, dear
Mademoiselle, lend my flowers some ideas. It has
always seemed to me that they ponder the void
through lack of education.

Saturday last, in Lausanne, I met Jaloux[1] and in the evening of my return I found on my table a long letter from Valéry: I was almost in France.

This week, by contrast, began sadly through the wild gusts which make of Val-Mont this Noah's Ark whose odd animals will certainly consume the olive branch proffered, taking it for medicament. The choice of those whom they will save from the flood has become extremely precarious in an ark where one pays; that other floating sanatorium of which God is doctor-in-charge was, I feel, surely better equipped.

I will probably have to absent myself next Thursday and Friday too: for this last day I promised myself to Jaloux, at least if the weather doesn't become too impossible. And then I reckon to complete my stay at Val-Mont, drawn out as insomnia, and whose secret ineffectiveness exasperates me. A thousand devoted thoughts.

R. M. Rilke

P.S. I add a little 'not' omitted in the final phrase of my last letter; that letter, I hope, no longer exists. Be aware then of my little posthumous 'not': and that it goes, afterwards, to rejoin the letter at its birth.

1 Edmond Jaloux (1878–1949), was a French novelist, essayist and noted literary critic. He was one of Rilke's key friends and contacts in the Parisian literary world and following the poet's death, Jaloux published a monograph on Rilke with Emile Paul-Frères in 1927. He also contributed along with Paul Valéry, André Gide, Romain Rolland, Maurice Betz and others to the honorary collection of essays *Rilke et la France* published by Plon in 1942.

LETTER 15

Val-Mont by Glion-sur-Territet

April 23rd 1926

A Friday! But I prefer the two others which
allowed me to wait for you, dear Mademoiselle.
Perhaps I could have come down today to
exchange words with you for a moment at the
door of your train carriage, if I had known I
wouldn't be in Lausanne, I would certainly have
had the immodesty to solicit this favour which
gave me the satisfaction to uphold the little tradition of Fridays . . . Feeling indisposed, I begged of
Jaloux to not await me until the following week. I
hope the coming one will be the last of my weeks
at Val-Mont, of which I have lost count.
Certainly, I will not leave here without having
announced myself to Dr and Madame Revilliod:[1]
'joyful and affirmative beings before life' . . . those

we rarely see; perhaps you yourself have also noticed, as I have, that I tend to side a bit with this rare belief. No one can agree more, and no one, I believe, can be more joyful before life than I was, me, at certain moments . . . imperceptible ones. For the real attachment to life means, it seems to me, to love . . . : *sein fast Unscheinbares, diese reinsten Gelegenheiten zu einem Glück, das so naturlich ist, dass die moisten an ihm, es nicht einmal gewahrend, vorüber-gehen . . .*[2] I think I have always replied with my entire being to these propositions without importance, capable, on occasion, to make us feel an incomparable accord. So much invitation exceeds us, disturbs us, or perhaps the extreme intensity where they draw us on scarcely allows us the anticipated correspondence. There is music which sets out on the highest note that we can yet conceive of and then what remains only offers us divine farewells . . . Throughout my whole life and since childhood, solitude was the most insistent educator who taught me this intimate attention; if suddenly it makes me fearful, it stems from this sudden disaccord between myself and my body . . . , without it, the clear Franciscan divide 'cella continuata dulescit',[3] adopted and approved so many times, will be forever more valuable for the retreat of Muzot. Might it one day reign once more!

And yet, what you say of the continuing ordeal that the silence of an isolated country house imposes is well known to me also, and I have borne the anxiety and peril at many times of my life. One starts out, in such a refuge, to establish some order, but one cannot keep order at all times. The temporary disorder, ignorance of oneself, the unconsciousness: so many elements of our perpetually moving form. These country houses are constructed rather in the sense that one can return to them. To return there from an anxiety-imbued and danger-filled existence, as Conrad did; to have lived life, a life so at odds with contemplation, and then, brimming with it, seething with it, and without yet even knowing if one will renounce this place entirely, (already!) to be seated in the same place where (before a fire playing its little drama upon the chimney) the ancestors reposed. Another danger of Muzot: to 'play', alas, these returns which are never made from a great-enough distance and fail to encounter an authentic hearth. To these returns, instead of remaining in repose, the imagination of the one who returns must provide everything: a past non-existent or foreign, and the incomplete present of the manor; with its own gesture, involuntarily, one would like to correct the deficit of a woman's gentleness and place certain things as she would have placed them. And the voice is saddened not to be heard by the dogs.

Gratitude for Lord Jim! I will not proceed here with this book of such richly filled pages . . . that will be for Muzot, for the summer. Thanks!

R. M. Rilke

(In Lausanne, a most curious exhibition of René Auberjonais.)[4]

1 A Dr Revelliod and his wife lived in Montreux at the time Rilke was at Val-Mont, so we can suppose with some confidence this was the person referred to.

2 'It's almost inconspicuous, these purest opportunities for a happiness, which is so natural that most people pass it by without even being aware . . .'

3 This reference to 'cella continuata' comes up several times in Rilke's correspondence of the period, most notably in an early letter from his incumbency on 7 October 1921 in which Rilke writes to his patron Werner Reinhart and enthuses over the magnificence of the surrounding countryside, the hot, dry climate which suits viticulture, the grandeur of the nights, and the sublime sunrises which remind him of those 'coming up over the Nile valley' and all this despite the 'hardness of his enduring cell', that is, the primitive confines of the Muzot tower.

4 René Auberjonais (1872–1957) was a prominent Swiss post-impressionist painter based in Lausanne.

Val-Mont by Glion-sur-Territet

May 3rd 1926

Dear Mademoiselle,

These few drops of alcohol have certainly fortified the 'very young tradition' (it's only the very
small dogs that remain small), and I thank you
for the result which, to be sure, was 'arduous'
only for your pen in the guise of a test tube. For
the recipient, this chemistry lesson had, let me
assure you, a most sensitive charm. Neither does
he, beginning once more one of these numberless
weeks of Val-Mont with a change of treatments,
neither does he write a proper letter to you this
time, his unchanging situation being irrelevant to
the better part of your fine questions. The arch
floats still and the doves anyway bring their sprig
of greenery.

Muzot calls me urgently, the masons have finished and I must decide on the paper with which they are going to line the walls of my study. Your counsel, so important for my 'room of greenery', I should have liked to invoke it in the same way with this room which was always green. With this ceiling with ancient beams of a very dark hue (beams dating from the 17th c.) what would you have placed there? In former times there must almost certainly have been wood panelling . . . It's all a bit too rustic and uneven to place any kind of cloth material there; I am going to have to resign myself once again to choosing some modern paper, the old ones simply cannot be found. Forgive me if I slip a small sample into this letter. Do you imagine it is possible to find this green paper which recalls that which was once there? The tone is pleasing and accords perfectly with the colour of the wood. Only, I would have liked to have done better, quite honestly, and to have chosen something which was more in keeping with the sense of this ancient room which is the one which I inhabit the most. On the walls there are only these 'stereoscopic views' of cities, time-worn and coloured, as one so often comes across.

My God, do please excuse me for dropping into your active life with these futile deliberations! I hope to be back at Muzot on Thursday (just for one day) to speak with the workmen; but if around the 10th, it might be possible for you to come by, I will do all to ensure that we might come back together!

Last Friday, eight days late, I had lunch in Lausanne with Jaloux: you can imagine that Paris was there with us and even Marseille! My nostalgia morphed into evocations during these amicable hours.

Geneva must be overflowing with light on these spring days, and the young ones to whom with so much care we endeavour to make the earthly proportions acceptable, I believe, find what sustains by approving them. I rather envy them your helpful and assiduous company.

R. M. Rilke

Val-Mont by Glion-sur-Territet

Vaud (Suisse)

First Friday in May

Dear Mademoiselle,

One sees that your cheerful babes demand no ink to 'overstimulate their dictionary' (as Valéry says). But it was so charming of you to stop the first pencil that comes along to address me these quick-fire lines. And you even found time to add to my little interrogatory sample this blond brother, who looks most engaging. But right now I allow myself the hope that pending any decision, you'll be able to counsel me next week, knowingly; for though I did make it into Sierre yesterday, it was far too cold, with a chance of snow. If your return to Sinneringen was not so urgent around the 15th, just think, what a god-send for Muzot! I will fix the date for my little trip only when you have let me know your plans and possibilities. I wouldn't go so far as to request that you make the slightest change to your current arrangements, but if a little free space happened to emerge between your disparate movements, know that the most sober Muzotien questions will gladly fill it!

I understood right away that you were saying that the doctors would leave me no hint of irony, not the least. Since my twenty-second year I nursed the happy ambition to employ personal means for the stabilization of my equilibrium; if one has exercised somewhat this interior hearing, so fine and with an infinitely precise perception, even nature itself rarely forgets to make its singularly native propositions in time. Only, for around two years, a malevolent magic (one of those tiny errors which gradually lead to huge deviations) has, so to speak, lead me into the enemy camp. A fine point of my instinct persists against my nature and unremittingly attacks this secret vital unity of 'me' that we can never quite reach but which unendingly reconstitutes itself. It is surely this intimate discordance that has delivered me up to the doctors. Delivered? Not exactly. In short, I am only attached like a qualified adviser, as with those navigators who, facing some maritime journey bristling with pitfalls, call out to the experienced pilot. Are there any potential experts, or is it a dimension never quite exploited, an unpredictable curve? And is it not almost a shame to be watched over in a perilous moment when all becomes 'questionable'? I have always thought that one stops, in some sense, the suspended hand of the saving angel, that we spoil his beautiful task by bringing in a rescue accomplice . . . and yet . . .

(Certainly, although the two reigns are not interchangeable, in such circumstances they leap from the bank of an ultimate thought over to almost an island thought, in action . . .)

Do you know, by chance, one or other of these young Genevans who were, body and heart, engaged in crossing the vast ocean in their yacht *Bonita*? My Zurich friends have spoken much recently of this candid and astute Mademoiselle

Maillart;[1] as for the name Mademoiselle Yvonne de Saussure, that has been pronounced often in quite other circumstances.

If, tomorrow, in passing, you happen to notice somewhere the May number of the *Nouvelle Revue Française*, please don't hesitate to bring me a copy: admirable annotations by Valéry. Drops (one could say) of transparent dew on his boundless verdure. What morning spirit!

R. M. Rilke

P. S. Do please hold on to the article attached to the *Tribune*.

1 Ella Maillart (1903–1997) and Yvonne de Saussure (1896–1935) were two of the five young women who famously crewed the yacht *Bonita* across the Mediterranean in 1925.

May 17th 1926

Dear Mademoiselle,

So it will be the 21st then that I'll have the joy of joining you on the train which comes by Territet at 10.13 for our Valais excursion! With this we grant time a final deadline to repent; perhaps it will come to its senses for the day of our little journey.

I have still not decided anything for the walls, I await your counsel, likewise for my garden, which is above all awaiting: your orders, dear Mademoiselle.

Last Thursday, I was with the Revilliods who treasure a warm memory of you. The hours I spent in their company were charming, I say 'hours', because after tea they retained me for supper and we chatted on endlessly.

If today I am also rushed, it's not, alas, that I must return to Alice i. W.,[1] but due to a multitude of letters (in all possible languages and even some reasonably situated between the different idioms) which have besieged me for days request and recall my pen from that walk to Morges which truthfully it would have preferred to any other form of exercise. I am overjoyed, Mademoiselle, to be seeing you this week and I thank you in advance for wishing to add another pearl to the necklace of traditional Fridays!

R. M. Rilke

1 Lewis Carroll's *Alice's Adventures in Wonderland* (1865).

LETTER 19

Dear Mademoiselle,

I said the same thing to myself a few days ago:
that one must defend oneself against that
persistent affluence of 'preconceived' thoughts.
Also I had held back a little from sending you
my modest packet from Montreux. It had, so it
seemed to me, the excuse of having been less a
sending of books than a simple and natural con-
tinuation of our conversation. Besides, it seems
that almost all our 'subjects' had been destined to
find a sequel, an immediate development, having
barely exited the bookshop, in front of a little
antique shop which had drawn them (as it had

once drawn myself on numerous occasions when I was shopping in Montreux), I encountered Monsieur and Madame Franzoni[1] and was content to lay out before them the proofs of my most recent recollections.

As for our conversations on Gide, nothing is easier than to pursue them further: for on my table, the two last numbers of the *Chronique des Lettres Françaises* lay waiting, of which one opened with an article by Jacques Rivière:[2] it was the text of a conference on André Gide that took place in Geneva in March 1918. I am fairly sure that it wasn't the conference you yourself heard and these pages which shed light on what we were talking about on Friday, in such a just and perfectly generous manner, surely deserve your attention one day; and I wait for you to suggest the follow-up article which will be presented in the next instalment of the *Chronique*.

This charming continuity of the greater part of our conversations, how could I not see it, a happy promise of relative permanence to this friendly interest that you have wished to take from my Muzotien concerns! My old tower somewhat tamed, doesn't seem quite so wild to you, in spite of its wretched disorder and its disorientated garden which rambles . . . In sum, we have visited a head whose mouth alone can summon a welcoming . . . , but what absence on the upper floor of this most ancient face, in the area of the eyes and of thought. (Note that with this distribution I indicate the dominant role which, if one chooses to remain with the image, would suit this rather dark but lucid guest room!)

What a shame then, through circumstances wholly interior, I am not, as it stands, one who would rejoice over an imminent return to this sturdy and peaceable retreat, for a while I would be . . . I am building myself some elder brother . . . Rightly, Madame de Noailles wrote to me saying I should love only the 'deepest fidelity'. What sorrow then to find marks of infidelity in the character, and still more towards a house to which I owe so much and which hasn't changed a bit!

In the patient wait to do better, a section of magnificent wall has just come into my hands which obliges me, of course, to choose a rather simple paper: you can be the judge: 'N 13069 (Michaud) Biographie Universelle ancienne et moderne / Paris, Michaud, 1811–1828; 52 vol, in 8, Octavo, bound in leather, a reddish-brown calf-skin, the rear blind stamped with gold, binding edge decorated with a lace pattern, marbled edges. Portraits. Superb example of the famous B.U., in a remarkably fresh romantic binding . . . .' How could I possibly resist?

I, who have a passion for lives lived more than any invention. And viewing it as a whole panel: 52 volumes, that really makes some display!

R. M. Rilke

Thanks for the Lausanne address; I am thinking of going there Tuesday or Wednesday.

1 The identity of this Monsieur et Madame Franzoni is difficult to establish. The poet, translator, literary critic and graphologist François Franzoni (1887–1956) visited Rilke in 1921 or 1922, accompanied by the historian and diplomat Carl Jacob Burckhardt. Franzoni also accompanied Antoinette de Bonstetten to Muzot on 21 May 1926 and another visit followed on 12 June. But Rilke may simply be referring to friends living in Montreux.

2 Jacques Rivière (1886–1925) was a leading French man of letters, writer, critic and, most significantly, prominent editor of *La Nouvelle Revue Française* until his death. He played a crucial role in recognizing Marcel Proust as a significant talent; engaged in a legendary letter exchange with the poet and dramatist Antonin Artaud; and also published works by Valéry, Romains and Giraudoux, among others.

LETTER 20

Dear Mademoiselle,

Wasn't it me who rather immodestly first employed the free rhythm of the intermittent epistolary? If it renounces the symmetrical order of politeness, it obeys far more interesting laws that I am more than happy to see you ultimately adopt.

Besides, this rhythm allows me to inform you of my return over the last fortnight. I am still residing at the Bellevue, but I go up twice a day to Muzot to keep an eye on the works there which advance with that charming Valaisan slowness; but which nevertheless advance, that is the principle. I might say that I have made myself into something of a young intelligent painter;

I traced in the air or on a scrap of paper all the movements which, little by little, descended upon the walls, and pursuing this method we are now in the act of creating an ensemble which I very much hope will gain your consent. We decided (after many a test run with the papers from Genoud) to paint the panels after my ideas on any background; especially we began to discover, in spite of all the irregularities common to architecture, all that is woodwork, and already by following this process we prepared a fairly clear frame that allowed us to work out the way it could be filled.

With that a deluge of mail! Imagine, a schoolmistress in a Bernese valley (Biembach p. Burgdorf) had read to her pupils a little story of mine from the past, and encouraged them to write to me: nineteen children thus wrote me nineteen letters, not so different it must be said, yet nuanced in a remarkable way. Here's the curious thing: in their slight awkwardness where an undaunted nature showed through, these little peasants and rustic types (who recounted to me the good news of the colour of their eyes!) spoke like kings or like the dead through their epitaphs. As for me, I am now obliged to compose nineteen different replies.

I knew that your next letter would bring me that Bernese address to which one would not like to concede too much reality! I have thought of you often, and to all these textbook farewells of which such a moving is composed. Its sadness must have been immeasurable! . . .

But, in truth, we only travel from one angel to the other; only, considering the measures and the distances of which they are accustomed to, it can sometimes seem to us rather exaggerated.

R. M. Rilke

P.S. I am sending you my copy of *La Bête du Vaccarès*[1] so that you can read it before me; I won't be able to engage with it anytime soon.

1 *La Bête du Vaccarès* was a novel by the Provençal writer and aristocrat Joseph d'Arbaud and was published by Grasset in 1926.

Hotel Hof-Ragaz (from which
I shall depart tomorrow)
Sunday 1st September 1926

So much have I thought of you: here, during my weeks of cure, and especially in this incomparable garden of 'Bothmar' in Malans.[1]—Awaiting the favourable moment for a letter, this beautiful book that J.-L. Vaudoyer[2] had sent me and which, here, was pretty much my only reading material! It dovetails with some of your memories and will make you (as it did for me too) some beautiful promises.*

R. M. Rilke

* J.-L. Vaudoyer, *Beautés de la Provence*, Paris 1926

1 Rilke refers to the baroque gardens of Chateau Bothmar situated above the village of Malans in the canton of Grisons which date from 1740–50 and are considered one of the most beautiful in Switzerland.

2 Jean-Louis Vaudoyer (1883–1963) was a prolific French novelist, poet, art historian, literary critic and regular correspondent with Proust. Vaudoyer's chief literary preoccupations were based on his experiences in Provence and Italy. The book Rilke mentions to de Bonstetten is *Beautés de Provence*, published by Grasset in 1926. Rilke had greatly admired Vaudoyer's *Les Delices d'Italie* (1924). Following their meeting in Paris in 1925, the two writers found they shared a deep love and knowledge of the landscape of Provence, echoes of which Rilke always found in the landscape around Muzot. At its publication in 1926, Rilke sent Vaudoyer a signed copy of *Vergers* to consolidate this mutual appreciation.

Hotel Bellevue

Sierre (Valais)

27th October 1926

You must, dear Mademoiselle, find inexplicable a
silence to which I was condemned after a run of
challenging circumstances. Barely returned to
Sierre, a wound and an infection have deprived
me for weeks now of the use of both my hands,
and the two were swathed in bandages. Just clear
of this unpleasantness, in Sion, where it was
doing the rounds, I promptly went down with
the gastric flu which confined me to bed until
yesterday.

But even before these incidents befell me, I
should have written to you on the subject of the
Muzot garden which of course you would not

have forgotten. Rather, I am the one who forgets! Even in the month of September, I had practically decided to call a halt to any further reorganization this year. There is now (just between you and me) something like a disharmony between Muzot and me, an ingratitude that I very much reproach myself for and that makes me, for now, flee the old house which oppresses me with a severity and solitude that I have felt ill-equipped to bear since my health has suffered. Added to this, I have the burgeoning desire to close Muzot up for the duration of the winter and to go in search of the south, the sun, the sea . . . ultimately something altogether different . . . I often muse on Saint-Cyr-sur-Mer! But at what time of the year might it be best to make a trip there, given the risks of combatting the mistral and all the inconveniences that come with a change of seasons? If I am not mistaken, you sojourned there last year, beyond the month of November? Are you thinking of making a return this coming winter?

I have so greatly regretted the loss of our meeting at Morges. What dispiriting days you must have suffered in Geneva, and on your return bringing back only mourning and pain. Have you read anything of the *Beautés de Provence*? I sometimes open this lived book as a way of keeping up with my winter projects. But all seems so terribly inconsistent after ten days of fever . . .

One of your fine lines will surely make me stand a little taller, the most consoling pleasure.

R. M. Rilke

Château de Muzot, nineteenth century, source unknown.